ANIMAL BEHAVIOR

Animal
Hunting and Feeding

ANIMAL BEHAVIOR

ANIMAL BEHAVIOR

Animal
Hunting and Feeding

NATALIE GOLDSTEIN

CHELSEA HOUSE
PUBLISHERS
An imprint of Infobase Publishing

Chelsea House
An imprint of Infobase Publishing
132 West 31st Street
New York NY 10001

Library of Congress Cataloging-in-Publication Data

Goldstein, Natalie.
  Animal hunting and feeding / Natalie Goldstein.
      p. cm. — (Animal behavior)
  Includes bibliographical references and index.
  ISBN 978-1-60413-143-7 (hardcover)
  1. Animals—Food. I. Title. II. Series.

  QL756.5.G63 2009
  591.5'3—dc22   2008040124

Chelsea House books are available at special discounts when purchased in bulk quantities for businesses, associations, institutions, or sales promotions. Please call our Special Sales Department in New York at (212) 967-8800 or (800) 322-8755.

You can find Chelsea House on the World Wide Web
at http://www.chelseahouse.com

Text design by Kerry Casey
Cover design by Ben Peterson
Printed in the United States
Bang EJB 10 9 8 7 6 5 4 3 2 1
This book is printed on acid-free paper.

All links and Web addresses were checked and verified to be correct at the time of publication. Because of the dynamic nature of the Web, some addresses and links may have changed since publication and may no longer be valid.

cover: An egg-eater snake swallows an egg from another animal's nest in Savannah, South Africa.

Contents

1

It's All About Food

IT'S NO SECRET that people love to eat. There must be thousands—maybe millions—of cookbooks that show how much we love food and how much time and energy we devote to making meals. No doubt, we are the only animal **species** that is so creative with food.

Lions may not savor a raw zebra flank the same way we relish the smell and taste of a perfectly cooked Thanksgiving turkey. Goats likely don't swoon at the delicate scent and velvety texture of a nibbled flower the way people savor their favorite desserts. Yet, all animals eat for the same basic reason: Food gives us the energy we need to stay alive.

Every human culture has its own food specialties. The type of food people eat and the way they prepare it has a lot to do with where people live. People who live in the far north hunt and eat fish and marine mammals because most plants can't grow in such a cold climate. People living in hot, humid places often eat spicy food. That's because spices help preserve food and keep it from spoiling in the heat.

Similarly, what animals eat depends on where they live. An animal's size and species also determine its diet. Both caterpillars and elephants feed on tree leaves, but they feed quite differently. There are many ways in which different animals can use a source of food.

WHY ANIMALS EAT

Everyone needs energy to stay alive. People use energy all the time, even when sitting or sleeping. Heart muscles keep blood moving through veins and arteries. Lungs take in and release air. Muscles and digestive organs are often at work, and the brain never stops working. Animals get the energy they need to stay alive from food.

The amount of food energy that an animal needs depends on how fast it burns, or uses up, the energy it has. The process of burning up energy is called **metabolism**. The more active a body is, the higher its metabolism. Moving muscles burn up more energy than relaxed muscles. The higher an animal's metabolism is, the more food it needs. A flying hummingbird beats its wings almost constantly. It has a very high metabolism and needs a great deal of food. Of course, an animal's size also determines how much food it must eat. Even a sleeping elephant needs more food than the most active hummingbird because the elephant has a much larger body to maintain. Also, warm-blooded animals maintain their own body temperatures, which requires energy.

A PLANETARY FEAST

Every living thing on Earth needs food to stay alive. All that food comes from one place: other living things. Almost every plant or animal is a source of food for something else. Animals not only need to find food, they also must try not to end up as a meal for another animal.

On average, hummingbirds flap their wings 50 times a second, which is faster than any other bird.

Most animals cannot eat just anything that comes their way. They are **adapted** to eating only certain types of food. A deer's teeth and digestive system are adapted to browsing tree leaves. A tiger's teeth, jaws, and digestive system are adapted to hunting and eating other animals.

When an animal eats food, chemicals called **enzymes** break down the food so the body can use it. A deer does not have enzymes to break down meat. So even if a deer ate meat, it would not get the energy it needs. If a tiger ate a ton of tree leaves, it would starve. That's because its stomach cannot digest and get energy from leaves.

WHERE FOOD COMES FROM

Where does food come from? This may sound like a silly and simple question, but it's not. The whole food circle of eating and being eaten always starts with the sun.

Sunlight contains energy. Green plants use this energy to make their own food. They do this by carrying out a chemical process, called **photosynthesis**. Plants absorb the energy in sunlight. They use that energy to chemically combine water (which their roots take in from soil) and carbon dioxide gas (which their leaves take in from the air). This produces a type of sugar. Plants use the sugar as food.

Green plants are the only living things that can make their own food. Because they do not have to eat any other living thing to survive, green plants form the foundation of the planet's food system.

Scientists have studied the feeding relationships among plants and animals. They have grouped every living thing according to what it eats. These groups are called feeding levels or trophic levels.

Green plants make up the first trophic level. They form the base on which all other living things depend. Because they make their own food and don't eat other things, green plants are called primary producers. That is, they produce the food (their own

Ecological Pyramid

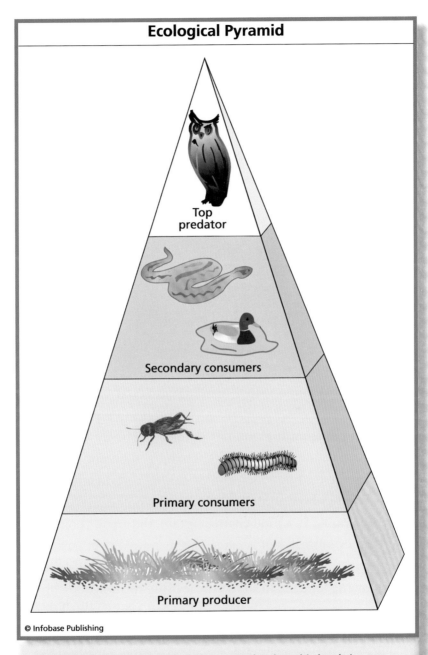

This ecological pyramid provides an example of trophic levels in one location. Reading from the bottom up, this example shows that grass and other plants provide food for crickets and caterpillars. Then they are food for snakes and small ducks, which in turn are meals for the owl.

bodies) that is at the base of all other food relationships. Without primary producers, no animals would exist.

Animals that eat green plants make up the next feeding level. These animals are called primary consumers. They consume, or eat, the primary producers (green plants). Primary consumers come in every shape and size, from insects to deer to elephants.

The next trophic level includes the first meat-eating animals. This group is called the secondary consumers. They eat the primary consumers. Secondary consumers include lions and tigers.

There can be several levels of meat-eating consumers. The highest level of meat eater is the top **predator**. The top predator can, and often does, eat any animal at any lower level. The top predator usually does not eat plants. Humans are top predators because they have the tools and the ability to hunt and eat all other animals. Humans are among the few top predators that also can eat green plants. However, humans are not always the top predator. People who go hiking in Glacier National Park in the Rocky Mountains lose their status as top predator to the grizzly bear.

Feeding relationships among animals can be shown in a diagram called a food chain. A food chain is a simplified picture that shows the feeding relationships among certain animals and plants. It shows how animals at different trophic levels interact with one another. In a food chain diagram, the arrows point from each plant or animal that is eaten to the animal that eats it. For example, in this food chain diagram, the weasel eats the hare. The following food chain shows the feeding relationships among plants, insects, and animals in a land **ecosystem** in which foxes, hawks, and owls are top predators.

Food chains are a simplified view of feeding relationships. A more accurate chart, called a **food web**, shows that most feeding

Food Chain

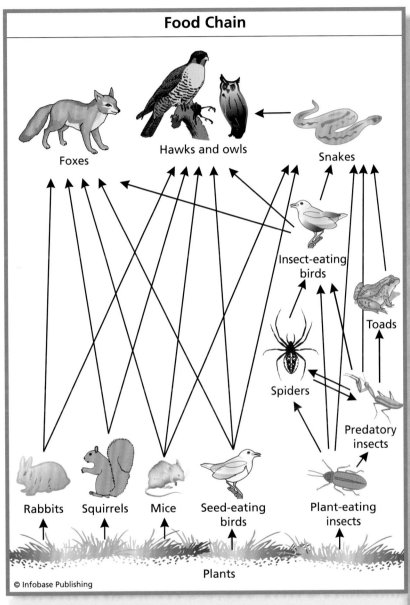

Foxes

Hawks and owls

Snakes

Insect-eating birds

Toads

Spiders

Predatory insects

Rabbits   Squirrels   Mice   Seed-eating birds   Plant-eating insects

Plants

© Infobase Publishing

The arrows in this food chain indicate how plants are eaten by herbivores, such as rabbits and plant-eating insects. They are then eaten by such carnivorous creatures as foxes and snakes.

relationships are complicated because they are not linear (e.g., one animal eats another who eats another) and they involve many more species. But even a food web doesn't show the whole picture. Most feeding relationships are so complicated that most people don't fully understand them.

2

Waiting for Food

SOME ANIMALS DON'T "work" for their food. They might plunk themselves down in one place for a long time and seem to do nothing. There's no reason to work hard to get food when it will come to you.

PASSIVE FEEDERS

Passive feeders wait for food to come to them. Many anchor themselves in one spot and wait for their meals to arrive. Passive feeding is possible only in places with rich food supplies. Most passive feeders live in water, particularly in the ocean along a shore. Near-shore ocean water is packed with food. Most of the food consists of tiny plants and animals that are carried by ocean currents.

These tiny **organisms** are called **plankton**. Algae are a common type of plant plankton. Some tiny animals (such as diatoms), the **larvae** of other sea animals, and even dot-sized water insects are kinds of animal plankton, called zooplankton. Coastal ocean water has so much plankton that it's like a rich soup of living things. The ocean is like a restaurant in which this soup is served to passive feeders.

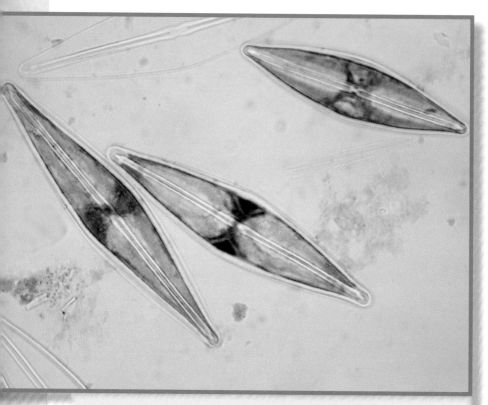

Diatom algae are a type of plankton found at the bottom of the marine food chain. Passive feeders eat the single-celled algae.

Filter Feeders

Sponges, clams, mussels, barnacles, and oysters are typical filter feeders. Anyone who has visited a rocky seashore at low tide has probably seen large clusters of mussels stuck to the side of a rock. Like most filter feeders, mussels will attach themselves to almost any solid surface that is regularly covered with ocean water. Barnacles also are known for sticking themselves to a solid surface, such as a rock or the side of a ship. They use a glue that they make themselves. Barnacle glue is made from several "adhesive" proteins that emerge from the barnacle's body as threads, as well as a material that makes the protein threads as hard as cement. Barnacle cement is the strongest (and most waterproof) glue in the world.

A filter-feeding animal attaches itself to a solid surface when it is young. Once attached, it stays put for its entire life. On this spot, the animal starts to grow. The soft, inner body gets larger. The animal produces a hard shell that protects it. Mussels and

Most filter feeders, such as mussels and barnacles (the white clumps attached to the mussels), attach themselves to a solid surface and stay there for life.

clams produce a two-part shell connected at one point. When an animal tries to eat a clam or mussel, the strong shell snaps shut. Only a few animals can open these shells to eat the tender flesh inside.

When the ocean tide goes out and they are exposed to the air, mussels and clams close their shells. This keeps their soft inner bodies from drying out. The shells stay closed until the tide comes in. When they are covered with ocean water, the mussels and clams open their shells to feed.

A filter-feeding barnacle eats by opening its many-plated shell and extending a fan of tentacles, or feathery limbs, into the water. The tentacles are covered with tiny hairs. They also are coated with a sticky, mucuslike substance made by special glands. As ocean water flows past, the tentacles are swept gently back and forth. Plankton get caught in the sticky mucus. Then the tiny hairs start moving, creating a gentle current of water that sweeps the food toward the barnacle's

Barnacle Feeding

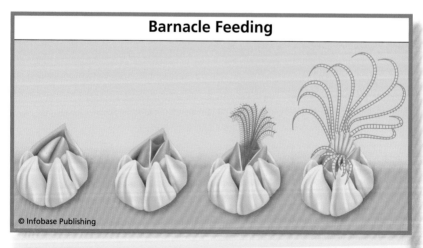

© Infobase Publishing

When a barnacle senses the tide returning, it opens its shell and extends its fan of feeding tentacles. When the tide goes out, the barnacle closes its shell again to keep it from drying out in the open air.

mouth. Each tentacle can snare hundreds of plankton during one feeding session. A barnacle keeps feeding in this way until the tide goes out. Then it closes up its shell and digests its meal.

A sponge is also a filter-feeding animal that lives stuck to one spot. A sponge gathers plankton by sucking in big "mouthfuls" of seawater. Then it strains the water through a strainer in its body. The strainer traps plankton. The rest of the water is released into the ocean.

Mussels, clams, and oysters have filter-feeding systems that use gills. When the tide comes in, an oyster's shell opens to reveal a fan-shaped structure that extends from the front to the back of the animal. The fan forms a gridlike screen projecting out into the water. As water flows through the screen, the mucus-coated, meshlike fan snares plankton. Tiny hairs on the screen sweep the plankton down "food grooves" on the tentacles toward the base of the gills. The gills screen out edible plankton, which the oyster eats. Food is moved through the oyster's gut by hairs similar to those on its fan. Unlike people, an oyster does not have muscles that move food through its digestive system.

Some filter feeders specialize in eating food that floats down to the sea bottom from the surface. These animals are called deposit feeders. Some kinds of shrimp, and many worms, are deposit feeders. Many of them burrow under the mud on the seafloor. When a burrowing shrimp is safe under the mud, it opens a part of its shell and extends two limbs into the water. The limbs move about, "feeling" for particles of food that have fallen onto the seafloor. When a tasty morsel is found and tangled in the limbs' mucus, tiny hairs on the limbs transport the food to the shrimp's mouth. Most sea worms use their tentacles to grope around the seafloor to find the remains of living things, or bits of organic matter. They use the tentacles, as well as mucus and tiny hairs, to catch and eat food.

Some filter feeders take a more active role in food gathering. Sea anemones are beautiful creatures that extend feathery tentacles into the water to catch food. However, sea anemones' tentacles have a food-snaring advantage: They contain stinging cells. These cells immobilize or kill prey that bump into the tentacles. The tentacle then carries the powerless prey into the sea anemone's mouth. Sea nettles and hydroids also "hunt" with stinging cells on their tentacles.

Floating Stingers

Sea anemones settle in one place for life. Jellyfish, on the other hand, float freely. But jellyfish are also passive feeders because they do not "look" for food. Jellyfish have long, threadlike tentacles hanging down from their dome-shaped, jellylike bodies. These tentacles are covered with stinging cells that can kill any prey unfortunate enough to come into contact with them. The sea nettle, a relative of the sea anemone, is a kind of jellyfish. Its body is a clear dome of a soft, jellylike material that is about 90% water. Nearly invisible tentacles extend from the dome into the water. They sway with the ocean current. The sea nettle's sting is powerful enough to stun or even kill a small fish or crustacean. When prey touches one of its tentacles, cells shoot out microscopically small darts filled with poison. The poison stuns or paralyzes the prey. The sea nettle then scoops it up and eats it.

A human swimmer who comes into contact with a sea nettle may get an unpleasant sting. Yet, this sting is nothing compared with the stings of larger and more poisonous jellyfish.

Not all jellyfish have stingers. The comb jellies are a group of jellyfish that use their dome-shaped bodies to pump

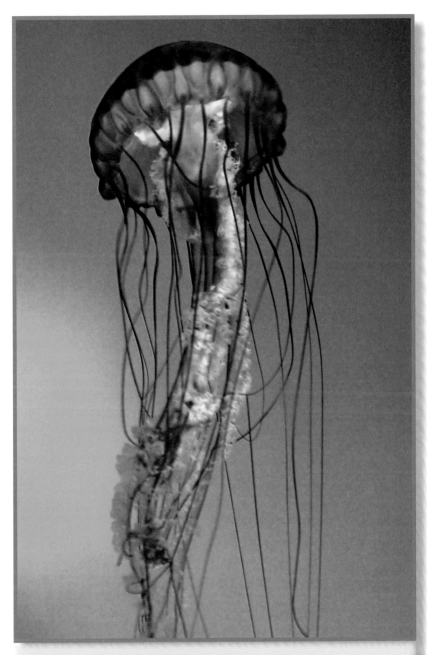

The saucer-shaped sea nettle mainly feeds on zooplankton and other jellyfish, but also eats small crustaceans and minnows.

water upward toward their numerous tentacles. When feeding, the dome expands and contracts in a smooth rhythm. This pumping action ensures that more food will be caught by the tentacles.

A flamingo is a filter feeder. Screenlike plates in its beak help it trap food in its mouth and let the water out.

FANTASTIC FILTERERS

Not all filter feeders are small marine animals. One of the most unique filter feeders is a large bird: the flamingo. A flamingo dips its head in the water and then turns it upside down. In this position, the bird uses its beak to filter tiny animals out of the water. A flamingo's beak contains plates that form a screen. The screen lets water flow through, but traps food. The flamingo sweeps its upside-down head from side to side through the water. The bird has a spiny tongue, too. Its movement helps pump water through the beak. When enough food is trapped behind the beaky screen, the tongue sweeps it farther back into the bird's mouth.

It's hard to think of a whale as a filter feeder, but some types of whales do feed this way. Of course, it takes an enormous amount of plankton to feed a whale, but these whales feed in plankton-rich waters. Filter-feeding whales are called baleen whales. Humpbacks, blue whales, fin whales, and right whales are baleen whales. Baleen is a filtering screen that baleen whales have in their mouths. The screen is made of horny plates with fringed edges that hang like a sheet from the whale's upper jaw. The baleen is pleated, so it folds easily when the whale closes its mouth.

A baleen whale feeds by opening its mouth and allowing the screen to expand. As the whale swims forward, it gulps in plankton-filled seawater. The water passes through the baleen, and the plankton are trapped in it. When the whale closes its mouth, the water is pushed out and the plankton are swallowed.

The fact that a two-ton whale can survive by filtering plankton out of seawater shows that the sea is rich in plankton. In Antarctica, a prime feeding site for some species, adult baleen whales routinely take in six to eight tons of krill—shelled zoo-plankton—every day.

TRAPS AND LURES

Truly passive feeding has its drawbacks. For example, not enough food may come the animal's way. Some animals seem to encourage prey to find them. They use traps or lures to tempt their meals to come to them.

Everyone is familiar with the most common animal trap: the spider web. Each species of web-spinning spider constructs a web with its own particular pattern. The pattern helps the spider trap the insects it likes to eat. After spinning its web, the spider sits and waits for an insect to blunder into the web. Spiders wait with each of their eight legs placed on a different web thread. This allows the spider to feel movement in all of the threads in the web. The spider waits for a tug that tells her that dinner has arrived.

In some spider webs, each thread is covered with dots of a sticky liquid. When an insect comes into contact with a thread, the "glue" traps it. As the insect struggles to free itself, it wraps itself in more sticky threads. Many spiders that spin sticky webs are immune to the "glue." The spider rushes across the web to check out its meal. Most spiders bite the struggling prey and use venom to paralyze it. The spider may then eat the prey immediately (by sucking out the fluids inside its body), or it may wrap the prey up in web threads and save it for later, when it is hungrier.

Not all spiders spin webs. The trap-door spider lives in the dry southwestern United States. This spider digs a hole in the sand and lines it with a type of silk, similar to the material in a spider web. Then the spider gets into the hole and begins to use silk and sand to make a covering, or trap door, over the hole. The

PASSIVE YOUTH

In a sense, the young of some animals feed passively. Baby birds must wait for their parents to bring them food. The young stay in the nest while the mother, father, or both parents look for food. Some bird parents bring whole foods, such as worms or bugs. Other bird parents eat food and fly back to the nest. The hatchlings open their mouths wide and cry out. The tiny open mouths and the cries trigger the parent to regurgitate, or bring up from its stomach, the food it has just eaten. Often, the young stick their tiny beaks into a parent's mouth to receive the regurgitated food, which is much easier for many baby birds to digest than chunks of food.

Some birds do not regurgitate food for their young. Owls, hawks, and eagles catch and kill small animals and carry them back to the nest. They drop the dead prey in the nest, and then it is up to the chicks to learn how to eat it.

Some young animals feed passively, like these baby blackbirds who are waiting for regurgitated food from their parents.

silk threads in the cover are connected to the silk within the hole, so when the spider is hiding patiently in the hole it can feel any insect touching the covering. The silk threads are so sensitive that the touch of even the smallest insect sets them vibrating. When the spider in the hole feels the vibration, it shoots its head out the trap door. It grabs the insect and drags it into the hole to dine on it. The trap-door spider moves so quickly that its prey has no time to get away.

Ant lions are desert insects. Before an ant lion burrows into the sand, it scoops out a little bowl in the sand. When the ant lion is satisfied with its bowl, it burrows under the sand at the bottom. Any ant that enters the bowl discovers that it cannot climb out. The sloping sides of the bowl are angled to prevent escape. As the ant tries to climb out, sand from the sides flows down over it. The more it struggles, the more trapped it becomes. When the ant lion hears the sand sliding down the sides of its bowl, it knows it's got a trapped ant. The ant lion emerges from its burrow and gobbles up the ant.

CAMOUFLAGE

Many animals that lay in wait for prey must blend into their surroundings to make sure they don't scare away an approaching meal. Blending into your surroundings is called camouflage. One of the champions of camouflage is the chameleon, a reptile that can change color to match its environment. Chameleons often sit still on tree limbs, waiting for insects to fly by. Chameleons stand stock-still as they swivel their eyes to see if a meal is approaching. When an insect nears, the lurking chameleon shoots out its fantastically long, sticky tongue and snares the insect. In the blink of an eye, the bug is snapped back into the chameleon's mouth.

Many insects, such as praying mantises, match the color of the leaves around them. These predators are nearly invisible

FLESH-EATING PLANTS

Bogs are places where the soil has very few nutrients. Bog plants must get the nutrients they need from somewhere else. Many bog plants have devised ways to lure, trap, kill, and digest insects. Because plants can't move around and hunt for prey, in some ways these plants are similar to animals that lure their prey.

(continues)

Flies and other insects can get stuck on the gluey substance lining the leaf pairs of a Venus flytrap. When something lands between the pair of leaves, the leaves will close around it to seal the trap, and the doomed insect will be digested alive.

(continued)

The Venus flytrap is probably the most famous flesh-eating plant. The plant's trap-door leaves are coated with a sticky substance. Its scent attracts flies and other insects. When a fly lands on a leaf, it becomes stuck. The plant senses that it has caught a meal. Slowly but surely, the leafy trap closes. The trapped insect is then slowly digested by enzymes.

Sundews are flesh-eating plants that attract flies to globs of gluelike liquid on their leaves. Any unfortunate fly that lands on a leaf and attempts to eat the glue is held fast. The trapped fly is slowly digested by the plant. Pitcher plants produce an insect-attracting liquid at the bottom of their slippery, tunnel-like leaves. Any insect that flies into the pitcher plant to feed on the liquid cannot escape. They are trapped by downward-pointing hairs that cover the slippery inner surface of the "pitcher." Eventually, the exhausted insect falls back into the liquid, where it dies and is digested by the plant.

and can catch any bug that wanders their way. (However, many insects use camouflage for protection from predators, too. For example, a stick insect that looks like a twig, and a leaf insect that looks like a leaf, are less likely to be seen and attacked by predators.)

The alligator uses camouflage as it waits for unsuspecting prey to approach. Floating just beneath the surface near the shore of a freshwater lake or river, an alligator is almost invisible. The alligator can see through the water. It keeps its eyes focused on the shore, where animals come to drink. When it spies a likely meal, the alligator charges out of the water with tremendous speed. Usually, the prey animal is so startled that it cannot react in time. The prey is quickly clamped between the alligator's powerful jaws. Alligators kill their prey by dragging it below the surface of the water and drowning it.

3

Sharing and Taking

GETTING AND EATING food is not always a fight to the death in which one animal wins and the other becomes a meal. Sometimes in nature two animal species help each other by the way they eat and the food they eat. A situation that benefits two animals of different species is called mutualism.

COOPERATION BETWEEN PLANTS AND ANIMALS

The most common form of mutualism is between plants and animals. Flowers produce **nectar**, which insects eat. While the insects are eating the sweet nectar, they also pick up pollen from the flower. As they move from flower to flower, the insects transfer the dustlike pollen, too. This is called pollination. Once a plant is pollinated, it can produce seeds, some of which eventually grow to become new plants. So plants benefit from this relationship, too.

There are less common mutualistic relationships between plants and animals. These relationships often involve insects. One type of stinging ant lives on acacia trees in Africa. The tree leaves produce nectar, which the ants eat. The acacia tree also produces thorns, in which the ants nest. The ants benefit from living on the acacia tree, and the tree benefits, too. If another animal tries to nibble the leaves of the acacia tree, the ants sting the intruder. The swarms of stinging ants protect the tree from animals that might eat its leaves and harm it. Both organisms benefit. In other parts of the world, ants that live on an acacia tree help keep other plants away. If a plant sprouts near the "home" acacia, the ants eat it down to the ground. These ants keep a large, plant-free border around "their" tree. This ensures that no other plant competes with the acacia for resources, such as water and soil nutrients.

There is a similar mutually beneficial relationship between corals and algae. Corals are animals that can't live long without the algae that live inside them. Corals live in shallow ocean water. They have soft bodies covered with cocoonlike shells that they make themselves, using a calcium-rich substance in the water. Corals live together in a community called a reef. Though coral animals do filter some food out of seawater, they cannot live on this food alone. So corals have algae living inside them. The algae carry out photosynthesis, which produces a type of sugar that the corals need to survive. The algae benefit because they live snug and protected within a coral's hard shell.

CLEANING UP

Some of the most amazing animal relationships occur between large, fierce predators and the small animals that help keep them clean. Cleaning fish, called wrasse, make their living picking food particles from between the teeth of sharks. When a shark sees a wrasse, it becomes a gentle dental patient. It opens its mouth and waits patiently as the wrasse swims inside and picks out bits of old food stuck between the many rows of razor-sharp teeth. The shark never eats the wrasse.

A rhinoceros peacefully walks while an oxpecker makes a meal of insects and other pests on its skin.

One species of shrimp waves its antennae back and forth through the water near a coral reef to attract fish. Any fish passing by is invited to stop and allow the shrimp to remove any food caught in its gills or any blood-sucking pests attached to its body. The fish appreciates getting a good cleaning and the shrimp gets the food it needs to survive.

Similar, mutually beneficial relationships occur among many other animals. The oxpecker is an African bird that lands on the backs of grazing animals, such as oxen, antelope, zebras, and cattle. The bird uses its beak to remove insect pests that have taken up residence on the skin of the grazer. Some of these insects make the grazing animals sick; others are just an irritant. In any case, the oxpecker pecks out the pests while the large animal grazes calmly. Again, both animals benefit because the grazer gets rid of infesting insects and the oxpecker eats the insects it craves as food.

ANIMAL RANCHERS

Strange as it may seem, some ants are the insect equivalent of cowboys or cattle ranchers. The ants don't actually raise cattle.

TOO CLOSE FOR COMFORT

Occasionally, two organisms become so dependent on each other that neither can survive alone. This is what happened on Mauritius, an island in the Indian Ocean.

The birds on this island had no predators. The dodo was one bird that thrived on Mauritius. Because it did not have to escape predators, the dodo lost the ability to fly. The dodo also developed a relationship with the tambalacoque tree, which grew on the island. This tree produced nuts with shells so hard that no animal could crack them open. Yet each nut had to be opened before it could grow into a tree. The dodo was the only bird that could swallow these nuts whole. Then, the bird's powerful muscles in its pebble-filled gizzard crushed the shell. When the seed was deposited on the ground in the bird's droppings, a tree would sprout.

Most people know that the dodo is most famous for being **extinct**. Hundreds of years ago, sailors who found Mauritius were delighted at how easy it was to catch and kill dodos. Ship after ship landed on the island so sailors

(continues)

(continued)

could slaughter hundreds, then thousands, of dodos, which were taken on board for food. It did not take very long for the dodo to become extinct. The last dodo was killed about 300 years ago. The only surviving tambalacoque tree on Mauritius also is 300 years old. No new trees have been able to grow since the dodo disappeared.

Dodo birds were the only birds on the island of Mauritius to feed on nuts from tambalacoque trees, and they deposited the trees' seeds through their droppings so that new trees could grow. Because dodo birds are now extinct, new tambalacoque trees do not grow on the island.

Their "livestock" consists of tiny nectar-sucking insects called aphids. The aphids punch holes in leaves and other parts of plants and suck out the sweet nectar. They digest it, turning it into a sugary substance called honeydew. Aphid-rustling ants love to eat honeydew. In this particular relationship, the aphids living on a plant provide honeydew for the ants. In return, the ants protect the aphids. They attack any invader, such as a ladybug, that tries to eat the aphids. The ants take good care of their "herd" of aphids. When the aphids are in danger, the ants "round 'em up" and move them to safer parts of the plant. They also "move 'em out" to young, fresh growth on the plant, where there is a good supply of nectar.

PARASITES

A parasite is an organism that uses another organism—a host—for its own benefit, even though this harms (or maybe even kills) the host. Almost every organism can be a host for one or more parasites. Some parasites spend only part of their life cycle with a host. For example, some flatworms enter a host mainly to feed for a while and lay eggs. The eggs are then released from the host's body, and develop outside the host. Other parasites, called obligate parasites, spend their whole lives dependent on a host. Tapeworms are obligate parasites that live inside a host's intestines. Tapeworms can live in humans. They feed on the food being digested. This reduces the amount of nutrients people get from their food. A person with many tapeworms might even die of starvation.

Botflies are one species of fly that parasitizes newborn birds. For botflies, timing is everything. Botflies deposit their eggs in birds' nests. The botfly eggs emerge as larvae just after a chick comes out of its egg. Then the botfly larvae burrow into the hatchling's body. The botfly larvae develop and grow

This sphinx moth caterpillar has numerous wasp larvae feeding on its body. It probably will not survive.

by feeding on the tissue inside the living bird. Infected chicks usually die.

Wasps use a similar strategy. A wasp lands on a caterpillar and injects its eggs into the caterpillar's body. When the eggs develop into larvae, they begin to eat the caterpillar. These caterpillars rarely survive. Usually, one species of wasp lays its eggs on only one species of caterpillar.

Despite the behavior of some parasites, such as those described earlier, it usually doesn't make sense for a parasite to kill its host. When the host dies, the parasite dies, too. Parasites that kill their hosts need a host for only a short period of time, not for their entire lives. Most often, parasites take as much as they need from a host without killing it.

Some parasites live outside a host's body. These parasites are often bloodsuckers. Anyone who's had a dog or cat with fleas has dealt with this type of parasite. Lice also are bloodsucking parasites. They sometimes affect people, taking up residence in their hair. Ticks are bloodsuckers that parasitize both animals and people.

Certain birds are nest parasites. The most famous nest parasites are cuckoos and cowbirds. A cowbird mother looks for the nest of another bird in which to lay one egg. Usually, the large cowbird egg is deposited in the nest of a bird that lays much smaller eggs, such as a warbler. After she lays the egg, the mother cowbird flies away. The tiny warbler mother does not seem to notice that she has one enormous egg among her own smaller ones. The warbler sits on all the eggs until they hatch. Fairly often, the cowbird egg hatches first. When this happens, the large cowbird chick uses it beak to tip the other eggs out of

FEARSOME BLOOD SUCKERS

A lamprey appears to be little more than a sharp-toothed circular mouth with a tail attached. Lampreys attach to fish and suck their blood. The lamprey's multiple rows of sharp, inward-curving teeth make it easy for the parasite to bite through the skin of a fish. Circles of suckers surround the teeth. They keep the lamprey firmly attached to its host's body. In the center of its circular mouth is the lamprey's tongue. The lamprey uses its tongue to stab at the wound it has made and suck out the fish's blood. A fish may survive having one lamprey attached to it, but will likely die if several of these creatures drain away its blood.

the nest. If the cowbird chick hatches at the same time as the warbler chicks, it uses its beak and its strength to toss or shove the newborn warbler hatchlings out of the nest. The mother warbler doesn't notice that anything is wrong! She will feed the cowbird chick as if it were her own. On rare occasions, a cowbird chick winds up sharing the nest with a warbler chick. But the larger cowbird chick demands, and gets, nearly all of the food that the parent warblers bring to the nest. The warbler chick usually dies of starvation. Nest parasitism has reduced the populations of some species of warbler and other small, rare birds.

Plant-Eating Animals

PLANTS ARE THE EARTH'S primary producers, and they grow just about everywhere on the planet. Wherever there are plants, there are animals that eat them. Every part of a plant is food to some type of animal.

FLOWERS, SEEDS, AND FRUIT

Flowers do not exist solely for the admiration of humans. Plants use flowers to attract pollinators. Many pollinators, such as bees, eat the sweet nectar that the plant produces deep inside each flower. As it sips nectar, a bee gets dusted with **pollen**. Pollen is made by the male parts of the flower. The bee carries the pollen to the next flower. There, the pollen falls on and fertilizes the female part of the flower. After fertilization, the flower produces one or more seeds.

Butterflies also are attracted to flowers. A butterfly drinks nectar through a long tube that extends from its mouth. Hummingbirds are nectar-eating specialists. Considering how tiny they are, most hummingbirds have very long beaks. Some beaks are curved; some are straight. The shape and length of a hummingbird's beak is adapted to feeding on specific types of flowers.

A hummingbird's long, thin beak allows it to sip nectar from the base of tube-shaped flowers.

Most hummingbirds sip nectar from long, tube-shaped flowers. The nectar is so far down inside the flower that only humming-birds, with their long beaks, can get to it. In some areas, such as rain forests, mice drink nectar. They also may pollinate flowers when they move from blossom to blossom.

Not all animals that visit flowers are after the sweet nectar. Some types of bees and beetles avoid nectar and eat the pollen. They pollinate the flowers as they fly from one to the next.

Most animals that feed on nectar or pollen also pollinate flowers. But some animals don't. They are called "nectar thieves." Nectar thieves can get to the nectar while avoiding the pollen. Some insects and birds, such as the Hawaiian honeycreeper, steal nectar by making a hole below the base of a flower. The animals suck the nectar through the hole without ever touching the pollen.

Anyone who has seen a squirrel knows that they love to eat tree seeds, or nuts. Nuts are seeds that are encased in a hard covering, or nut shell. Nuts contain nutrients meant to feed the sprouting plant as it grows. Many types of rodents, including mice and chipmunks, also eat nuts and the seeds of other plants.

Blue jays are birds that help spread nuts over a wide area. The birds collect nuts in the fall. They bury them in the ground to save them for the winter. They bury far more than they can eat. Often, a blue jay may forget where it buried some of its nuts. In spring, these forgotten nuts may sprout into tree seedlings.

Parrots and other birds also love to eat nuts, but they scatter them in a different way. A parrot swallows an entire nut, but may digest only part of it. After a while, the nut **kernel**, or seed, is expelled in the parrot's droppings. The droppings act as fertilizer for the kernel, which may grow into a new tree.

Most plants produce far more seeds than will ever grow into new trees or plants. This way, at least a few seeds will take root and grow. Some plants try to "protect" their nuts and seeds from being eaten by animals. For example, some kinds of bean plants produce seeds that contain nasty-tasting or poisonous chemicals. Other plants have seeds with sharp spines or

Squirrels can crack open the hard shells of nuts with their sharp front teeth and can grasp the nuts with their paws.

irritating fuzz on them. Still other plants encase their seeds in shells that are so hard, it's difficult for most animals to break them open.

Animals that eat seeds and nuts have adapted to overcome some of these obstacles. Squirrels have strong, sharp front teeth that can chip away the hard shell of most nuts. Their paws can easily hold onto a nut as they nibble it. Parrots have sharp, strong beaks for breaking nutshells. But some nutshells are so hard that no teeth or beaks can crack them. Animals often eat these nuts whole. Digestive enzymes break down the tough shell and then digest part of the seed or kernel. The seed is dispersed with the animal's droppings and may grow into a new plant.

Some plants protect their seeds by surrounding them with fruit. Fruit not only protects the seed in the center, it attracts animals that will eat the fruit and aid in dispersing the seed. A fruit consists of a mass of usually sweet, juicy flesh surrounding a central nut, which has a shell protecting the seed inside. Most fruits are brightly colored. The color of the fruit tells the animals when it is ripe and ready to be eaten.

Many animals love to eat fruit. As their name suggests, fruit bats fly through the forest, looking for trees that have the ripest fruit. In some African rain forests, elephants are the main fruit eaters. Sometimes the elephants pull ripe fruit off a tree with their trunks. But most of the time, elephants eat fruit that has fallen onto the ground. Much of this fruit was probably dropped by fruit-eating monkeys. A monkey will grab a fruit, eat part of it, and then drop it before reaching for another one. The monkeys' "bad habits" are a boon to elephants and other animals. Many animals wait below a monkey-filled tree for half-eaten fruit to fall. These animals generally can't climb trees, so the rain of partially eaten fruit is a treat for them.

Fruit has its disadvantages as a food item. Though it is tasty, fruit does not contain all the nutrients that most animals need

A fruit bat needs to eat more than fruit, so it will also eat flowers and pollen of fruit-bearing trees—though this one is biting its nails. Fruit bats' long claws allow them to hang upside down from trees to survive. Fruit-eating animals must eat other foods. Fruit bats eat the flowers and pollen of fruit-bearing trees. Some monkeys, birds, and other fruit-eating vegetarian animals also eat nuts or other plant parts to get the nutrients they need. Some fruit eaters, including many monkeys and apes, also will eat meat when they can get it.

GRAZERS AND SHRUB-MUNCHERS

When people think of plant-eating animals, many think of animals such as deer, cattle, buffalo, horses, sheep, goats, and zebras. Animals that feed only on plants are called herbivores.

Animals that eat grasses and other low-growing green plants are called grazers. Horses, buffalo, sheep, goats, zebras, antelopes, wildebeests, and many similar animals are grazers. Grazers eat the leaves, stems, and flowering parts of many types of plants, including grasses and grains, legumes, and wildflowers.

ROOTERS

The roots or root parts of plants are food for some animals. A gopher is a burrowing animal that uses its long, strong front teeth and forelimbs to tunnel out its home under the ground. Gophers feed on plant roots, bulbs (short plant stems and buds encased in fleshy leaves, as in tulips), tubers (fleshy stems containing plant buds, as in potatoes), and runners (very thick underground roots that can sprout into new plants). Gophers rarely eat enough of a plant's root to kill the plant.

Porcupines are also fond of the underground parts of plants. They supplement their main diet of leaves and fruit with tubers and roots they dig up out of the ground with their strong, **dexterous** front paws.

Animals that eat the leaves off trees are called browsers. Deer and moose are browsers. Most browsers eat mainly tree leaves, but sometimes they also will nibble on grasses and other low-growing plants.

Grazing and browsing animals have special teeth to tear plant tissue and grind it down before they swallow it. Grinding teeth are wide and flat. They look something like human molars, but are much more powerful. A deer's grinding teeth are exceptionally wide. They have curved ridges for cutting up tough plant fiber. A deer can even chew up tree twigs. Like many browsers, deer have no top front teeth, but they don't need them. A deer uses its powerful tongue to hold food against the roof of

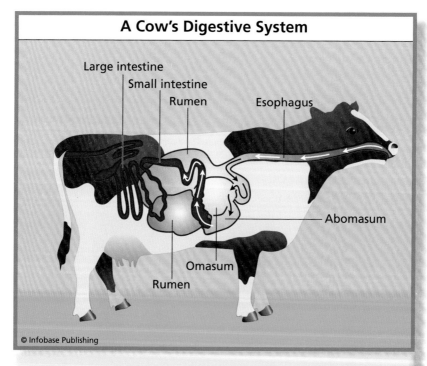

A Cow's Digestive System

Large intestine
Small intestine
Rumen
Esophagus
Abomasum
Omasum
Rumen

© Infobase Publishing

A cow's stomach has four chambers. Each chamber contains different bacteria that help break down and digest plant food. After plants are eaten, the nutrients in them are available for the cow's body to use.

UNWELCOME HERBIVORES

Leaf miners are just one type of plant-eating animal that can do real damage to a plant. Leaf miners usually are insect larvae. A mother insect makes a hole in a leaf, and then deposits her eggs. When the eggs hatch, the larvae begin to tunnel through the leaf, eating as they go. The leaf provides the miners with both food and protection. The tracks of most leaf miners are easy to see. Some birds may seek out leaves with mining larvae, but most animals avoid them.

Nearly every part of a plant can be infested with miners or borers. Some insect larvae bore through the stem of a plant or the bark of a tree to eat the tissue inside. A healthy tree or plant can usually weather a mild infestation of borers or miners. However, a young or stressed plant may die if it is heavily infested.

its mouth. Then it slices through the plant tissue with its sharp bottom front teeth. Its tongue moves the food back toward the grinding molars.

Plant food is difficult to chew and digest. Think about it: For plants to stand upright, they must be made of strong material. This tough plant material is called cellulose. Browsers and grazers need large, strong grinding teeth to break down cellulose. They also need special enzymes and bacteria in their digestive tracts to digest it. Plant food is so difficult to digest that some animals eat the same food twice. When a cow "chews its cud," it is re-chewing food that has already been chewed and swallowed. A cow bites off some plant food and then chews and swallows it. After the food spends some time in its stomach, the cow brings it back up into its mouth and chews it some more. A cow will bring up cud and re-chew it with its strong grinding teeth until it can digest it. Then it swallows the food for the last time, and the food moves through the cow's digestive tract.

SAFETY IN NUMBERS

Almost all grazing and browsing animals live and feed in a herd, or group. There are many reasons for living in a group. One is protection: the larger the group, the less likely it is that any one animal will become a meal for a predator. In a herd, some of the animals are always on the lookout for predators. When one member of a herd spots a predator, it lets other herd members know by giving a warning signal of some kind. Then, the herd members usually run away. If a predator attacks, the members of the herd may run in different directions. This behavior tends to confuse the attacker and lessens its chances of making a kill. Living and feeding in a herd offers greater protection for vulnerable youngsters that would otherwise be easy pickings for hunters. Herds also allow animals to take advantage of a food source when it is at its peak. Instead of individual animals wandering around looking for food, all of the animals can exploit the best food at the same time.

The Hunters

LIFE AROSE ON EARTH more than three billion years ago. The first life forms were single-celled blue-green algae that sloshed around on the surface of the sea. These organisms made their own food using the energy in sunlight. They didn't have to worry about being eaten. But then a change occurred. Some of the single-celled organisms lost the ability to make food. They had to look elsewhere to find nourishment. The only food available to them was the blue-green algae. They developed a variety of ways to hunt for and consume the algae.

Some of these ancient hunters are still with us today. The amoeba is a single-celled organism that hunts other single-celled organisms. The amoeba has no definite body shape. It moves by streaming: It changes its shape by creating and extending "false feet" (pseudopodia) that move it forward. When it comes into contact with another single-celled creature, an amoeba begins to trap it. The shape-shifting amoeba extends false feet that wrap themselves around the prey. Soon, the prey is surrounded by the amoeba. The amoeba then takes they prey into its body and digests it.

HUNTERS THAT DON'T KILL

Some hunters do not kill the prey on which they feed. Just about everyone has been prey for a mosquito. Mosquitoes seek out warm-blooded prey, such as humans, and land on them in order to drink their blood. The mosquito makes a tiny hole in the prey's skin and withdraws blood. It uses the blood to feed itself and its **offspring**.

Vampire bats are commonly featured in horror movies as the ultimate scary predators. Though vampire bats do look frightening, they are among the least harmful of the world's predators. Like almost all other bats, vampire bats hunt at night. They hunt for warm-blooded animals. Using two hollow, razor-sharp fangs, a vampire bat makes tiny holes in a prey animal's skin. Then the bat sucks blood until its hunger is satisfied. Most of the time, vampire bats don't seriously harm their prey. A bat bite rarely, if ever, kills the prey. A prey animal gets a small bite, but it may be harmed only if the bat that bites it carries a disease that it may transmit to the prey.

FINDING PREY

Most animals must go looking for food. One of the first rules of successful predation is knowing where to look. It helps to know a prey's habits. Large predatory mammals know that their prey need to drink water. So for lions and other predators, waiting for prey near a water hole is a good hunting strategy. Predators also learn when particular prey animals come to drink, so they are waiting at the right time.

A successful predator observes and learns about the habits of its prey. Birds that eat caterpillars know that their prey can be found on the leaves of a particular species of tree at a certain time of day, and only when the leaves are new and fresh. This helps birds zero in on the right trees at the right time.

WAITING TO BE EATEN?

Considering that the whole world is one big restaurant, it should come as no surprise that some predators hunt and eat passive feeders. Sea slugs, which are mollusks, eat a variety of passive feeders. They slowly make their way over coral reefs, using their pumplike mouths to suck the coral animals out of their shell-like cocoons. Sea slugs also feast on sea anemones. They are not hurt by the stinging cells on the sea anemone's tentacles. In fact, sea slugs eat the tentacles. They then incorporate the stinging cells into cells on their back. Sea slugs use these stingers to repel predators.

Parrotfish also feed on coral animals. Parrotfish use their powerful beaks to chip away the hard cocoons.

Starfish use the suckers that line each of their five arms to pull apart shellfish, such as mussels and clams. While a clam remains stuck to a solid surface, the starfish grabs each side of its shell with an arm. The starfish uses its powerful muscles to pull the shell apart. Then it eats the animal inside.

A parrotfish has a powerful beak, which is useful for cracking hard cocoons to get the coral animals inside them.

Using Senses

Animals learn about the world the same way as humans do—they use their senses to understand their environment. Though all animals have the same five senses that people have (and some have more than five), most predators use one, or maybe two, highly developed senses to find and catch prey.

Sight

When a person is said to be "eagle-eyed," it means that he or she has amazingly sharp vision. Eagles and hawks soar high above the land, floating on warm masses of air called thermals. The thermals keep them aloft; they don't need to use energy flapping their wings. As they float on the thermals, eagles scan the ground below for prey. An eagle or hawk can identify a small mammal, such as a rabbit, from more than a mile away. Once the bird spots its prey, it swoops down toward it. As a hawk nears its target, it extends its long, powerful talons. It grabs the prey and lifts it into the air. Eagles and hawks carry their prey to a high spot, such as a rock on a mountainside or a nest in the top of a tall tree. Holding the prey with its talons, the eagle or hawk rips away bits of its flesh with its powerful beak.

Most big cats also have highly developed vision that they use for hunting. Lions skulk around water holes, their eyes glued to the herding animals that come there to drink. Lions, and similar large predators, use their eyes to analyze the fitness of the different animals in the herd. They're experts at spotting a prey animal's weakness, such as old age, extreme youth, or lameness. Anyone who has a pet cat knows that cats have acute eyesight. A cat can detect the slightest movement that might betray the location of a prey animal. Once a cat spots a mouse or bird, it watches the prey with intense concentration.

Birds such as swifts and swallows swoop through the air in graceful flight that seems, to the human eye, to be quite random. Actually, these birds are preying on insects. They can spot insects flitting through the air and change course to catch them on the wing.

Visible light is only a small part of the entire electromagnetic spectrum. Some animals can see light waves that are invisible to humans. For example, bees have keen vision in the ultraviolet range, where light waves are shorter than the light we can see. Flowers that are pollinated by bees often have ultraviolet "guidelines" on the petals that humans cannot see. But bees can see these guidelines, and they follow these pathways into the flower to eat the nectar.

Pit vipers probably deserve the prize for "super-normal" vision. Below their eyes, pit vipers have two pits that contain heat-sensitive membranes. The membranes can "see" infrared (short wave) images at night. Infrared images change depending on the temperature of an object: A cool object gives off less infrared radiation than a warm object. As a pit viper slithers along the ground at night looking for prey, it uses its infrared vision to "see" the heat given off by a prey animal, such as a mouse. The snake's infrared vision is so acute that it can sense a temperature difference to within a few thousandths of a degree. Once a prey animal is detected, the snake silently slinks up to it and devours it.

Taste

Pit vipers and other snakes also can "taste" the air. When rattlesnakes famously flick out their forked tongues, they are literally tasting the air around them. Each snake has a pouch on the roof of its mouth called a vomeronasal organ, or Jacobson's organ, that can recognize the "taste" of a nearby prey animal. The snake's flicking tongue picks up particles in the air and then carries them

A rattlesnake can use its tongue to taste the air for nearby prey. This Mojave rattlesnake in Arizona is in a defensive posture.

to the pouch. A sensory organ in the pouch tells the snake if prey is nearby.

Scent

Many animals hunt using their keen sense of smell. A wolf can smell a prey animal, such as an elk or a moose, from more than one mile away. Weasels and similar small mammals also use their keen sense of smell to find food.

Polar bears use their acute sense of smell to recognize the breath of a seal emerging from a hole in the Arctic ice. A polar bear can smell a seal's breath from more than three miles away, even if the seal hole is buried under three feet of snow. Once the polar bear catches the scent, it uses its sense of smell to find the seal hole. The bear will wait patiently near the hole for a seal to poke its nose out. Then the bear grabs it with its long, sharp claws, drags it onto the ice, and eats it.

Deep ocean water may not seem like the best place to detect odors. Yet sharks have such an acute sense of smell, they can smell blood that's miles away. Only a few drops of blood in the water will do it. The shark's brain identifies the odor and signals "food" to the shark, which seeks out the bleeding prey.

Hearing

Owls are among the most sharp-eared hunting animals. In addition to having acute hearing, owls have ears that can move to hear sounds coming from any direction. An owl can hear an insect moving through blades of grass at night. It can hear the footfalls of a mouse on the ground. When it detects prey, an owl takes flight. Its wings are shaped and feathered in such a way that they make no noise. The silent owl swoops down on its prey and grabs it with its talons. Then it carries off the prey to eat it.

Bears have poor eyesight, but keen hearing. In several national parks in the western United States, hikers are advised to wear bells in remote parts of the park, where bears live. If a hiker suddenly appears in front of a bear, the bear may panic and attack. The bells allow bears to hear approaching hikers while they are still far away. Usually, the sound of a bell will send a bear scurrying away. This may not be a great way to see a grizzly bear, but it's a fine way to avoid being attacked by one.

One of the champion sound-hunters is the desert-dwelling, fox-like fennec. A fennec's ears are nearly half the size of its body. It uses these enormous ears to help cool its blood

The giant ears of a fennec help it hear potential prey.

during hot desert days. It also uses its ears to find food. A fennec's hearing is so acute that it can hear a beetle moving in a hole underground. It can hear the movement and even the breathing of a gerbil in an underground burrow. The fennec hunts with its head down and its ears turned toward the ground. When it has located prey, the fennec uses its powerful front legs to dig up its dinner.

Touch

Passive hunters use touch to find food on the ocean floor. Among fish, touch is a common means of detecting prey. Fish have a line of highly sensitive cells that run lengthwise along their bodies, from gills to tail. It's called the lateral line. The cells in the lateral line are sensitive to changes in water pressure. Just as waves

BOUNCING SOUND

Bats and dolphins are in a class by themselves when it comes to using hearing to find food. Both types of animals use **echolocation** to locate objects. When an insect-eating bat leaves its cave for its nighttime hunt, it gives off high-pitched bursts of sound. The sound waves travel through the air until they hit an object. Then they bounce back to the bat. The bat detects the echoed sound waves using a special organ. This organ tells the bat how far away the object is, what type of object it is, how big the object is, if the object is moving, and in what direction it's moving. When a bat detects a tasty insect on the wing, the bat sends out faster pulses of sound. This helps the bat zero in on the insect. The folds and flaps of skin on a bat's face are adaptations that help it receive the echoing sound waves.

Dolphins, too, use echolocation to find prey, and to orient themselves under water. Dolphins emit high-frequency clicks. When they detect prey, they start sending out more clicks: as many as 500 per second. Dolphins have a sensory organ that interprets the echoes. The organ tells them the location, size, and speed of the prey.

Both bats and dolphins use sound waves at high frequencies that human ears cannot hear. To people, it seems that these animals are silent, even though they are making a high-frequency racket.

form around a stone thrown into a pond, waves form when a fish swims. These waves create the slightest change in water pressure. A fish's lateral line detects these changes. Fish can tell whether the changes come from prey or some other source. If it's prey, the fish will swim in the direction of the pressure change, looking for the prey.

THE RIGHT WEAPONS: HUNTING TOOLS

Finding prey is a great start, but it doesn't mean much if an animal cannot catch, kill, and eat the prey. Predators have a wide variety of "tools," or physical adaptations, which help them feed.

Teeth and Fangs

Plant-grinding herbivores have broad, flat teeth. Carnivores—animals that eat only meat—need teeth for killing prey and ripping apart their flesh. Just about all carnivores have fangs: long, pointed incisor teeth. Wolves, coyotes, and dogs; lions, tigers, and cheetahs; foxes and fennecs; bears; and even insect-eating rodents, such as the short-tailed shrew, have fangs for sinking their teeth into and then ripping apart a prey animal.

Mammals are not the only predators that use fangs for hunting. Venomous snakes have long, sharp, hollow fangs that are attached to poison-producing glands. When the snake strikes a potential prey, it sinks its fangs into the animal. Venom flows through the fangs to paralyze or kill the prey. The fangs of the monstrous viperfish, which lives on the cold, dark ocean floor, are intended to impale any prey that may have the misfortune to wander near it. The viperfish has fangs on both its upper and lower jaw. The tips are hooked to keep prey from getting away.

Predatory spiders, such as tarantulas, have fangs, too. Like snakes, the tarantula's fangs are hollow and deliver a dose of paralyzing poison. Black widow spiders have venom so strong that it can kill a human. Yet the bite of a black widow is nothing compared with that of the funnel web spider of Australia. This spider's venom is one of the most powerful of any animal in the world. If a person is bitten by this spider and not

The viperfish has a hinged jaw, which enables it to eat large prey.

treated immediately, death from heart failure occurs in about two hours.

Aside from fangs, other carnivore teeth contain ridges and points that help these animals tear apart their fleshy food. Incisors, premolars, and molars each have a function in cutting, slicing, ripping, or pulverizing fresh meat.

Brute Force

Sharp fangs and flesh-ripping teeth would be useless if a predator did not have a jaw powerful enough to sink those fangs deep into its prey and hold on. Most predators have jaws strong enough to crush a prey animal's windpipe, to snap its spine in two, or even to crush its skull. The jaws are strong enough to allow the hunter to drag the prey – which in some cases weighs hundreds of pounds—to a quiet area, where it can eat in peace.

If prey animals are not killed instantly, they will fight to save themselves. Hunting animals must be strong to win these struggles. In addition to large jaw and neck muscles, most predators have powerful leg muscles to either chase or restrain prey. Pythons are snakes with powerfully contracting muscles throughout their bodies. A python will kill prey by wrapping itself around an animal and squeezing. The animal either suffocates because it can't expand its lungs to breathe, or it is crushed to death. Then the snake eats the prey whole. A python is able to swallow a small deer in one long gulp. Anacondas also kill prey this way.

Claws, Talons, and Beaks

Predatory birds have talons; predatory mammals have claws. Most claws and talons are made of the same stuff as human fingernails, though they usually are much harder and sharper. Mammal claws and bird talons generally curve downward. When the predator clamps down on prey, the claws or talons curve into the flesh for a better hold. In some mammals, claws can be drawn back into flaps of skin on the paws.

Some seashore and marine animals also have claws, or pincers. Many species of crabs have a pair of claws with spiny edges. The spines help the crabs hold onto prey. The sharp tips of the claws allow crabs to rip apart prey. Lobsters live on the seafloor, and they also have pincers that they use to capture and shred prey.

Bird beaks come in a variety of shapes and sizes, depending on the diet of a particular bird species. Swifts and swallows have long, thin beaks for spearing and eating flying insects. Birds of prey, such as hawks, have strong, hooked beaks for ripping

A black skimmer fishes by skimming its larger lower beak through the water.

"FISHING" FOR BUGS

Chimpanzees are smart and agile. They have learned how to prepare a plant stem and use it as a tool to hunt termites. Making a "termite-fishing rod" is not as easy as it may sound. Chimps are very particular about choosing just the right type of stem for termite hunting. They prepare the stem by removing its leaves. Then the chimps carefully insert the "fishing rod" into a small hole in a termite mound. When the chimps slowly withdraw the stem, it is covered with termites, which the chimps promptly nip off with their lips. The process is repeated until the chimp has eaten its fill.

This procedure may sound simple, but it's not. Scientists who have studied the chimps and tried to do their own termite fishing failed miserably.

This female chimpanzee is preparing a stick to use as a tool in fishing for termites.

apart animal flesh. Woodpeckers have thick, pointed beaks suited to hammering holes in tree bark in their quest for grubs and insects.

Fish-eating birds have a variety of beaks, too. Herons have long, pointed beaks that allow them to spear small fish in shallow water. An oystercatcher's beak is powerful enough to hammer open an oyster shell. A black skimmer's beak is unusual. The lower beak is longer and wider than the upper. The black skimmer flies low over the water with its mouth open and its lower beak "skimming" the water. When the larger lower beak scoops up a fish, the bird quickly closes its mouth and eats its prize.

HUNTING BEHAVIOR

For a predator to succeed, its prey must be unaware that it is about to become a meal. Patience is necessary. Stealth—moving secretly and almost invisibly—is also required. Lions and other big cats stand stock-still as they watch potential prey. When a lion moves in on a prey animal, it inches forward silently. At the right moment, the lion lunges with power and ferocity. The element of surprise is key.

Owls also use patience and stealth when hunting. An owl waits until its prey is in an open area where it can be easily caught. The owl's silent wings allow it to scoop up the prey before the animal realizes what's happening.

Most predators rely on patience and stealth, but a few do exactly the opposite. The European stoat, a kind of weasel, weighs only about 0.6 pounds (0.3 kilograms), but it hunts rabbits that weigh 10 times as much. A stoat creeps through the grass until it's near a rabbit. Then it suddenly sits up and begins to "dance," leaping up and down and swirling around as if chasing its own tail. The stoat does somersaults and back flips. The rabbit sits transfixed. While the rabbit is frozen in wide-eyed amazement, the stoat leaps at the rabbit and sinks its teeth into the back of the rabbit's neck. This cracks the rabbit's skull, killing it. A stoat can feast on one rabbit for many days.

No matter how stealthy a predator is, it must reveal itself when it begins to attack its prey. Once a predator reveals itself, prey try to run away. So speed is important for hunting success. Wolves can run as fast as 20 miles per hour (32.2 km/hr) in pursuit of prey, but they can't sustain this speed for long. If a wolf decides that it will not be able to catch a prey animal, it gives up the chase to save energy for the next try.

The cheetah is a relatively small "big cat" that lives in Africa. The cheetah is the fastest land animal in the world. It can run at a speed of 70 miles per hour, although it cannot maintain this speed for long.

There are so many examples of interesting feeding behaviors among predators that there isn't space to describe them all here. But here are a few examples. Some types of sea gulls eat mussels and other shellfish that are protected by thick shells. The gulls' beaks are not strong enough to break open the shell. So the gulls fly high into the air with a shell and then drop it onto rocks. The impact cracks open the shell. Then the gull lands next to the broken shell and eats its meal.

Otters that live in the ocean are marine mammals that enjoy crabs, oysters, clams, and other shellfish. A sea otter cannot crack open these shells by itself. A hunting otter always has a rock tucked securely in its armpit. When it finds a shellfish, the sea otter floats on its back and lays the rock on its stomach. Then the otter grabs the shellfish with both "hands" and slams it against the rock until the shell is cracked open.

The ferretlike mongoose uses a related tactic to crack open the eggs that it steals for food. It throws each egg on the ground, like a child bouncing a ball. Once an eggshell is smashed, the mongoose can eat the nutritious food inside.

A sea otter can easily eat clams and other shellfish by smashing them open. Sometimes it will even swim carrying a rock under its armpit, so it can use the rock to smash shells.

For quite a while, people thought that no animal could hunt and kill a porcupine. Wildlife biologists now know that there are predators that have learned how to overcome the porcupine's painful quills. Fishers, bobcats, and wolverines can kill porcupines. The predator creeps up on a porcupine, lunges at it, and flips the porcupine onto its back. Before the porcupine can right itself, the predator rips open the porcupine's soft belly with its claws.

SNAKES UNHINGED

A snake is able to swallow eggs and animals much larger than itself because it can unhinge its jaws. Most species of snake have a hinge between their upper and lower jaws. When a snake catches large prey, it uncouples the hinge. Then it opens it mouth around the prey. The snake's upper jaw is ridged with teeth, and the right and left sides of the jaw move independently. The snake uses its upper teeth to grab onto the prey. Then the snake moves each side of its jaw forward, bit by bit, over the prey. In this way, the snake "walks" its jaw over the prey until the animal is inside its mouth. Then the prey makes slow progress down the snake's throat toward its stomach. Muscles along the snake's throat help push the prey down.

Snakes—like this corn snake that is eating a mouse—unhinge their jaws and essentially "walk" them over their prey in order to swallow them whole.

MAKING THE KILL

Most prey animals, especially small ones, are eaten alive. Snakes, insect-eating birds, many fish, and a host of other predators simply swallow their living prey whole. Pelicans are water birds that have enormous pouches under their lower bills. When a pelican has filled its pouch with small fish, it simply swallows the still-squirming mass in one gulp.

Larger prey usually cannot be eaten whole or alive: they are too big and too powerful. Even a relatively small mammal will fight and struggle to fend off a predator. Most predators kill larger prey before beginning to feast on it.

Big cats kill their prey quickly. A cat will bring down a prey animal by leaping onto its back, sinking in its claws, and then dragging the animal to the ground. Once the cat has the prey down, it clamps its powerful jaws around the animal's neck. This action quickly crushes the prey's windpipe or breaks its neck. The prey is killed instantly.

Wolves, African wild dogs, and hyenas take much longer to kill prey. These animals hunt in packs. They surround and subdue a prey animal. Sometimes, wolves will use their powerful jaws to break a prey animal's neck prior to eating it. But most often, they eat their prey alive. A pack of wild dogs or hyenas surrounds the prey and pulls chunks of flesh off its body, usually beginning with its hindquarters and legs.

Cooperation: Group Hunting

Though most animals are solitary hunters, some animals are more successful hunting in groups. Some hunt in groups for safety reasons. Penguins feed in groups because there's safety in numbers. It's less likely that an individual will be killed by predators if there are many other penguins around. However, penguins do not cooperate to catch fish. Each penguin fishes alone.

Some animals do cooperate to catch prey. Wolves, wild dogs, and hyenas hunt in packs. Female lions, called lionesses, cooperate to bring down large prey, such as buffalo or zebras. They spread out in a line over a fairly wide area in which they know that prey will appear (for example, around a watering hole). Crouching low in the grass, the lionesses inch forward toward a herd of prey, watching them intently. At some point, one of the lionesses determines that a prey animal is in a good position. She leaps out of the grass and charges. The panicked prey begins to run away from the charging lioness. But the hunt is planned in such a way that as the prey flees the charging lioness, it runs into the other lionesses. The waiting lionesses attack and kill the prey.

Most cats hunt alone. But cooperation among hunting lionesses improves the cats' hunting success. A lion or other big cat that hunts alone will have one successful kill for every seven attempts. When lionesses cooperate, they catch prey one out of every two attempts. Of course, lions that hunt together must share their meal, while a lone lion does not have to share. Still, the greater success of cooperatively hunting lionesses must make this behavior worthwhile.

Generalists and Specialists

THERE ARE SOME animals that will eat just about anything. Most people, for example, eat a wide variety of foods. People are omnivores: animals that do not specialize in eating one type of food. People can eat meat, as well as many kinds of plants. People can't digest grass and other tough plant products, but the human diet is filled with variety.

Although having a varied diet might seem to be an advantage, most animals are not omnivores. They have evolved digestive systems that can handle only meat or only plants, but not both.

One of humans' closest relatives, however, is an omnivore. Chimpanzees are apes that eat mostly leaves, nuts, and fruit. They also eat termites, which they "fish" for using special sticks. Yet, when chimps crave meat, insects just won't do. Chimps love meat, and they actively hunt and eat small animals, such as lizards. They also steal eggs from birds' nests. From time to time, a group of chimpanzees may have a hankering for a real meat meal that impels them to search out other game. One of a chimpanzee's favorite foods is the flesh of other monkeys, particularly the red colobus monkey.

Chimps live and hunt in groups. A group of chimps will cooperate to hunt colobus monkeys. Several large male chimps climb up near a group of colobus monkeys feeding calmly in the treetops. The chimps surround the monkeys on three sides. Then they attack. The colobus monkeys cannot climb down because female chimps are waiting for them. So the colobus monkeys rush through the treetops in the only direction open to them. There, another large male chimp is hiding among the leaves. This high-ranking male grabs the first colobus monkey he can, and uses his powerful jaw to break its spine. When the rest of the chimps see the successful kill, they scream in excitement. The male carries the colobus monkey down to the forest floor, where all the chimps will share in the feast.

Another omnivore may be much more familiar to people. A raccoon will eat just about anything. Raccoons eat seeds, nuts, fruit, and other plant parts. They also hunt for worms by listening for the rustling sound created as they move through grass or leaves. Raccoons also love small fish, shellfish, and frogs. They will spend hours near a stream, using their humanlike hands to try to catch food.

Raccoons' hands can manipulate objects precisely and they are very sensitive. Raccoon hands are so sensitive that a raccoon can tell if a fruit is ripe or not just by touching it. A raccoon can pull a delicate worm from its hole without damaging or breaking it.

Raccoons also use their hands to get into things they shouldn't. Most adult raccoons can easily open garbage cans and select delicacies that humans have thrown out. Raccoons have been known to open doors and let themselves into houses, where they look for food. People have found a raccoon standing in front of an open refrigerator door, peering inside like a child choosing a snack. Luckily for humans, raccoons cannot pick door locks.

Brown bears are probably the largest of all omnivores. In the spring, their diet consists largely of plant food, such as grass, tasty roots and tubers, and skunk cabbage. In summer, they will feast on all sorts of berries. Brown bears supplement their vegetable diet by digging up mice, squirrels, and marmots from their burrows. Bears have six-inch long claws and powerful arms, so digging up these small animals is a cinch for them. If a brown bear

Raccoons will eat just about anything—including potato chips.

lives near the seashore, it may also wander down to the beach to dig up small animals buried in the sand. The brown bears that live in Yellowstone National Park have developed a taste for cutworm moths, which eat wildflowers. During the day, the moths sleep under rocks. Unearthing the moths is no problem for the bears. Bears will climb thousands of feet up into the mountains to devour moths, eating as many as 30,000 a day.

Brown bears are huge animals. An adult male may weigh 1,000 pounds. They also are strong and fast. A brown bear easily can outrun a human. Brown bears use their large size and immense strength to hunt and kill mountain sheep, moose, and deer. Because a bear uses so much energy pursuing these prey, they are not a regular part of its diet.

The most famous bear-feeding scenes occur in Alaska. There, Alaskan brown bears gather along the Mackenzie River, among other rivers, to eat salmon. The salmon swim up the rivers from the oceans to spawn, or mate. The bears form groups near small waterfalls and rapids. Here, salmon must leap out of the water to continue their swim upstream. Despite its poor eyesight, a bear uses its dexterity and perfect timing to grab a leaping salmon with its large claws or with its mouth. Bears also wait near shallow water and catch salmon as they swim by. Bears are usually solitary creatures, but during this time of the year, dozens of bears may gather at one spot to fish. There is so much food available that the bears rarely fight.

Sometimes an animal that normally is not omnivorous becomes so when living around people. In the wild, sea gulls eat fish or shellfish. As humans have moved in on the gulls' natural **habitat**, the birds have learned to take advantage of human leftovers. Gulls are a common sight at landfills, or garbage dumps, that are close to rivers or seashores. The gulls will eat just about any food that people have thrown away.

DIFFERENT FOOD FOR DIFFERENT AGES

Frogs are one of the only animals that change their diet as they mature, or grow older. A young frog, called a tadpole, eats only plant food. Its mouth and digestive system make it a strict vegetarian. As the tadpole matures into an adult frog, its body changes dramatically. The adult frog's body is adapted to eating insects, which it snares with its long tongue. The adult frog cannot eat plants. In the natural life cycle of a frog, the animal changes from being an herbivore to a carnivore.

Tadpoles, or young frogs, are herbivores. When they mature into adult frogs, they become carnivores.

SPECIALISTS

In contrast to omnivores, feeding specialists can eat only one type of food. An herbivorous specialist can eat only one type of plant. A carnivorous specialist eats meat from one type of animal.

Giant pandas are one of the world's most famous and beloved specialists. Pandas live in the bamboo forests of China. They eat only bamboo, which is a type of giant grass. Bamboo is one of the toughest plants to eat. Its stem is strong and woody. It can grow 50 feet tall. The panda has evolved large, flat molar teeth to grind down this tough material. The panda also has a unique finger, similar to a thumb, which allows it to grab the bamboo stalk so it can chew on it like celery.

Koalas are tree-living Australian animals that eat the leaves of eucalyptus trees. These trees also are called gum trees. The leaves contain poisons that would kill most other animals. A koala's digestive system is immune to the toxins. Not only is the koala immune to the leaves' poison, but it also is one of the only

The toothless anteater eats ants using its long, curved snout and its even longer tongue.

MEERKATS VS. SCORPIONS

The meerkat is an endearing, weasel-like animal that lives in one of the harshest environments on earth: the Kalahari Desert. Food is very hard to come by in this hot, dry habitat. Animals that live here have adapted to eating things that other animals would avoid.

Meerkats eat scorpions, which are relatively common in the Kalahari. Scorpions, which are related to spiders, have one of the most poisonous and deadly stings of any animal in the world. However, meerkats have devised a way to hunt and eat them. When a meerkat finds a scorpion, it bites off the dangerous stinger at the end of its tail. Then the scorpion is defenseless, and the meerkat can eat it. Sometimes, meerkats do get stung. Though the sting is painful, the meerkat has developed a resistance to the powerful poison. It will not die when it is stung. The sting may keep the meerkat from eating this particular scorpion, but soon it will be fine and hunting its deadly food again.

In order to eat a scorpion, a meerkat will bite off its stinger. Though they sometimes still get stung, meerkats have developed a resistance to the stingers' poison.

animals with a digestive system adapted to get nutrients from eucalyptus leaves.

There are other animal specialists. One is the snail kite, a bird that feeds on one species of snail. Another is the anteater, which feeds only on ants and termites. The anteater has no teeth. Instead, it has a long snout and a long tongue. At night, when the ants are asleep, the anteater uses its powerful front legs to break into an ant nest. As the sleepy ants try to discover who or what has broken into their home, the anteater slurps them up. The anteater will eat hundreds of ants from each nest it invades. Ants are not that nutritious, so anteaters don't have much energy. An anteater spends most of the day curled up on the ground, sleeping. It is kept warm by its large, furry tail, which it drapes over itself like a blanket.

LIFE ON THE EDGE

When a habitat is stable—its plants and animals are thriving, its weather is normal, and there are no disruptions—specialist animals do well. However, specialists are vulnerable to changes in their environment. For example, koalas are an endangered species because human development (buildings and roads) and wildfires have destroyed large numbers of eucalyptus trees. Being dependent on a single source of food can lead to starvation if that food source disappears. Sometimes, a specialist animal can adapt to eating a different, though similar, food. Too often, though, when a specialist's food disappears, it starves. The species may even go extinct.

Giant pandas are highly endangered because humans have destroyed their bamboo forest habitat. Yet, pandas always have been vulnerable. All bamboo plants of the same species flower at the same time. After they have produced flowers, the mature bamboo plants die. Bamboo plants may flower only once every

Specialist animals, like koalas, depend on a single food source. Koalas are endangered because they depend on eucalyptus trees, which have been destroyed in large numbers due to human activity and wildfires.

15 years, or even once every 100 years. But when a particular species of bamboo produces flowers and dies, it poses a serious problem for pandas. Once all the mature bamboo plants have died, the pandas might have to migrate to another part of the bamboo forest, where a different species of bamboo is still available. Even in the best of times, this is a serious problem for pandas. Today, with the added pressure of human development and a much smaller forest in which to find food, the pandas are in serious trouble. If China's population and development continue at today's pace, the giant panda may become extinct in the wild.

Animals such as the giant panda, which resembles a large, furry teddy bear, are easy for people to care about. That's why "adorable" animals are the best known of the endangered specialists. But, in fact, most endangered specialists are insects and the plants on which they feed. In tropical rain forests, some plants can be pollinated by only one species of insect. If one of these species of plants is destroyed when the rain forest is cut for farming or logging, the insect that feeds on this plant's pollen or nectar may disappear, too. If pesticides kill all or most of this species of insect, the plant cannot be pollinated and may go extinct.

This type of relationship occurs in the deserts of the southwestern United States, where each species of yucca tree can be pollinated only by one species of yucca moth. If human activity destroys one yucca tree species, then the moth that feeds on it also will disappear. If one species of yucca moth dies out, the species of tree that it pollinates also will die out.

Not all endangered species are feeding specialists, but many are. Feeding specialists live "on the edge," meaning that they are always at greater risk for extinction or a population crash, compared with animals that have a varied diet.

Scavengers and Decomposers

SOMETIMES CHILDREN ARE told to "clean their plates," or eat everything they were served. In the wild, predators don't eat every morsel of prey, but nothing is wasted. Many animals "clean up" leftovers or break down organic material, which can then be used by other living things.

SCAVENGERS

Scavengers eat dead prey instead of killing and eating live prey. They may eat the remains of prey left over by predators. They also may feed on the bodies of animals that have died of other causes. Hyenas and vultures are two common scavengers.

Scavengers have a bad reputation among some people because they feed on dead animals. Yet, they provide a necessary service in the natural world. Dead bodies rot and attract disease-causing organisms, such as certain bacteria. If scavengers did not consume most of the remains of dead animals, their rotting bodies could contaminate the land and nearby water sources. Scavengers manage to speed up the process of decay by ripping flesh into smaller bits that are more easily broken down.

Hyenas and vultures are both scavengers that feed on dead animals. This spotted hyena in Kenya is chasing away vultures from the meal it found.

Hyenas are one of the most common scavenging mammals. Though hyenas do hunt and kill prey themselves, they also feed on the leftovers of other predators, especially lions. Hyenas pay close attention when lions are on a hunt. If many lions surround the kill, the hyenas will wait for them to abandon the prey. Then the hyenas move in to feed on what's left. Sometimes, though, only one or two lions may be feeding on a kill. If the hyena troupe is large, it may continually harass and attack the lions until the large cats give up their meal to the hyenas. They will feed on parts of the prey that lions don't eat.

Hyenas do lots of "clean-up" work in their native Africa. On that continent and in almost every other part of the world, vultures or similar birds feed on dead animals, which also are called carrion. Vultures have keen eyesight; like eagles and hawks, they keep a lookout for a meal far below. Vultures also watch one another. When one vulture heads for the ground,

OUR NATIONAL SCAVENGER

When the Founding Fathers discussed which bird should represent the United States, many opposed using the bald eagle. Though it is a magnificent-looking bird, it has some habits—such as feeding on carrion—that some of our early leaders found offensive.

Benjamin Franklin thought that choosing the bald eagle as our national bird was a terrible mistake. He suggested the turkey. Though the turkey has many wonderful qualities, people did not feel that it looked the part, and the bald eagle supporters overrode Franklin's opinion.

Many people were opposed to having the bald eagle represent the United States because it is a scavenger. It typically uses one talon to hold its prey and one to stay on its perch as it tears off pieces of dead prey with its beak.

other vultures know that it has found food. They follow. That's why it seems that in the blink of an eye, a mob of vultures appears at the site of a dead animal. Other scavenging birds, such as marabou storks and griffons, will watch and follow vultures. One vulture swooping toward a fresh carcass will start a chain reaction in which other scavenging birds and land animals all head for the dead animal. Even predators take advantage of the "I found food" signal provided by a descending vulture. Lions and other predators will feed on animals that have died of natural causes.

Most vultures feed on a dead animal's soft tissue, such as muscle and organ meat. Some vultures specialize, feasting only on skin and tendons, for example. All vultures and most other scavenging birds have strong, sharp, curved beaks for tearing flesh. Some vultures have long necks that allow them to delve deep inside a carcass to pull out organs.

Animals compete for carrion. A large group of feeding vultures may be chased from their meal by a lion. The vultures wait patiently for the lion to eat its fill. When the lion leaves, the vultures move in again. However, they may be chased away again, this time by marabou storks. These birds can grow to more than 5 feet (1.52 meters) tall, with a wingspan of more than 8 feet (2.44 meters). Instead of a curved beak, a marabou stork has a long, straight bill that can dig into a carcass and rip out large chunks of flesh. Small vultures feeding on carrion will be displaced by large vultures, large vultures by marabou storks, marabou storks by hyenas, and so it goes. Usually, each scavenger leaves some food uneaten, so there's generally a meal left for a variety of carrion-eating animals.

Animals die in every habitat—and other animals are there to make meals of them. At the seashore, crabs are one of the most abundant carrion eaters. Crabs use their claws to pull off and eat bits of a dead animal's body. On the seafloor, lobsters often

When it comes to feeding on carrion, marabou storks can displace large vultures, but can also be displaced by hyenas. These marabou storks in Masai Mara, Kenya, are feeding on a carcass with their long, straight bills.

scavenge. The bodies of dead animals decay rapidly in watery environments. Here, deposit feeders are important actors in the breakdown of carrion.

DECOMPOSERS

Organisms that break down dead bodies or waste are called decomposers. Insects, worms, bacteria, fungi, and microscopic organisms are among the world's many decomposers.

Soil Organisms and Their Role in Decomposition

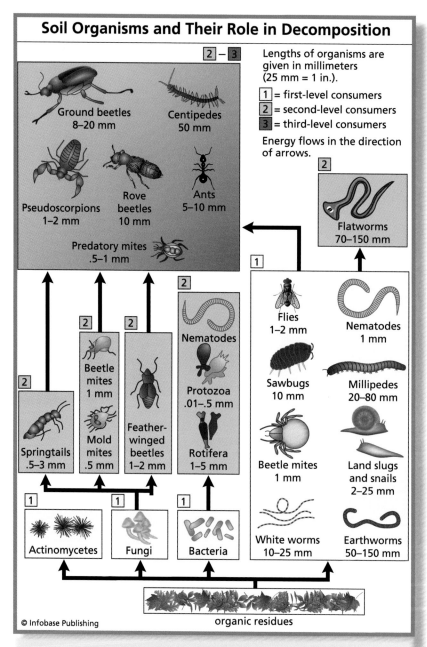

2 – 3

Lengths of organisms are given in millimeters (25 mm = 1 in.).

1 = first-level consumers
2 = second-level consumers
3 = third-level consumers

Energy flows in the direction of arrows.

Ground beetles 8–20 mm

Centipedes 50 mm

Pseudoscorpions 1–2 mm

Rove beetles 10 mm

Ants 5–10 mm

Predatory mites .5–1 mm

Flatworms 70–150 mm

Springtails .5–3 mm

Beetle mites 1 mm

Mold mites .5 mm

Feather-winged beetles 1–2 mm

Nematodes

Protozoa .01–.5 mm

Rotifera 1–5 mm

Flies 1–2 mm

Nematodes 1 mm

Sawbugs 10 mm

Millipedes 20–80 mm

Beetle mites 1 mm

Land slugs and snails 2–25 mm

Actinomycetes

Fungi

Bacteria

White worms 10–25 mm

Earthworms 50–150 mm

organic residues

© Infobase Publishing

Many organisms on and under the ground help break down dead organic material into nutrients. Plants take in these nutrients through their roots. Herbivores eat the plants, predators kill the herbivores, and the cycle continues. Decomposers are vital in keeping the nutrients that organisms need cycling from soil to plants to animals and back again into the soil.

Decomposers break down animal and plant tissue. They also break down the leaves that fall in autumn until they become a part of the soil. Leaves and other organic material are composed of many substances, including nitrogen and proteins. As different decomposers "work on," or eat, dead organic matter, they release nutrients into the soil. Decomposing organic material is so widespread that decomposers have their own complex food chain.

After scavengers have completed their work, decomposers take over part of the task of breaking down organic tissue. Flies lay their eggs in decaying meat. Fly larvae, or maggots, feed on the rotting flesh. While maggots feast, bacteria grow on the carcass. The bacteria feed on the carrion and release nutrients. Other bacteria, insects, and fungi—such as mushrooms—decompose the flesh that is in contact with the soil. These organisms consume the flesh and—using enzymes—break it down into nutrients. Each type of organism feeds on dead material and breaks it down into one or more parts. Some of the first decomposers turn dead plants or animal matter into sugars or starches. Later on, other decomposers will break down tissue into nitrogen, proteins, and other nutrients. Each decomposer has an important role to play.

Some decomposers specialize in the breakdown of dead animal tissue. Others, including many types of fungi, specialize in breaking down dead plant tissue. In any forest, there are dead trees lying on the ground. Many have fungi growing from them. If a person touches the dead tree, wood-eating insects may scurry from beneath the rotting bark. Microbes also are at work, breaking down cellulose and other hard-to-digest parts of the tree. Beneath the tree's trunk, millions of decomposers, including insects, worms, and microbes, eat and digest the organic material. Digestion breaks down the plant tissue, which is then incorporated into and enriches the soil.

Decomposition of dead organic matter takes place in every environment. However, some conditions are better for

This log is from a tree that died and fell in the forest. The fungi growing on it break down its tissues. Insects and microbes also digest and decompose the decaying log, which eventually will become part of the soil.

decomposition than others. Warm, wet environments speed up the process. Cold or dry environments slow it down. A hiker is more likely to find animal bones in the desert than in a rain forest.

Animal waste is another important food source for decomposers. Most animals don't absorb all the nutrients in the food they eat. Their waste products contain leftover nutrients. Some insects and microbes spend their lives breaking down animal feces into organic particles and nutrients. Plant-eating animals—such as horses, sheep, cows, and chickens—produce feces, or manure, that is chock-full of nutrients. Manure makes great fertilizer: It enriches the soil and helps to grow healthy plants. That's why farmers and gardeners work manure into the soil in which they grow vegetables and other food. Plants can't grow in "pure" manure. Manure must become part of the soil.

ALL THAT EARTHWORMS DO

Earthworms occur in almost every type of soil on earth. In temperate regions, there may be hundreds of earthworms in each square yard of soil. Some people think that earthworms are "icky." These people may not know that all land-based life owes its existence to earthworms.

Earthworms move through the soil ingesting organic matter. As food moves through an earthworm's gut, it is digested and then eliminated as a nutrient-rich substance that enriches the soil. Earthworms also allow air to circulate through soil. As they wiggle their way down from the surface, earthworms create "air tunnels" that allow air to move deep into the soil. This speeds up decomposition, so

(continues)

(continued)

"airy" soil is richer in nutrients and organic matter. Also, by churning up the soil, earthworms prevent it from becoming compacted. Scientists say that without earthworms, it is likely that the soil could not support plants. It would be too heavy and compacted for roots to grow. It also would not have the air that roots need to function properly, and it would have too few nutrients to support plant life. Because all life depends on plants, the land might be lifeless without earthworms.

Earthworms are important for keeping soil rich with nutrients. As they feed on organic matter, they leave behind nutrient-rich substances for the soil.

Worms, insects, and microbes break down the manure, and its nutrients are released into and mixed with the soil. Plants absorb the nutrients they need with their roots.

Agents of Change

SINCE THE FIRST blue-green algae floated in the oceans billions of years ago, life on Earth has evolved to produce all of the plant and animal species that exist today. Over billions of years, various species of organisms have existed. Over time, as conditions changed, they also changed or disappeared. The dinosaurs are probably the most famous of all ancient extinct animals. They dominated every landmass for millions of years. Many scientists believe that dinosaurs died out when an asteroid (a large rock from space) about 6.2 miles (10 km) wide struck Earth about 65 million years ago. Scientists believe it may have landed in Mexico because a crater of a similar size (about 112 miles, or 180 km, in diameter) and age was found there in 1991. The impact of the asteroid would have caused an earthquake 1,000 times more powerful than any ever recorded. Nearby seas would have boiled, and winds from the shock would have reached nearly 250 miles per hour (400 km/hr). Most likely, a tsunami swept around the globe, and dust particles may have blocked out the sun for years. All of these effects, as well as others, changed living conditions so dramatically that dinosaurs (and many other animals) could not survive.

It does not take a natural disaster, such as an asteroid impact, to cause plant and animal populations to change, or evolve.

Changes can occur because of feeding relationships, such as the close interaction between a predator and prey, or intense competition for limited food resources.

The process of **evolution** describes how species change over time. It is also the process by which new species are created. Evolution is driven by two factors: changing environmental conditions and random changes in an individual's genes. Genes are the parts of cells that pass on traits from one generation to the next. Offspring inherit many of their parents' traits. For example, human children get genes from their parents that affect hair color and eye color, height, foot size, nose shape, whether or not the child has dimples, and many other characteristics. Most plants and animals inherit traits in the same way.

The genes an animal gets from its parents may make it more or less likely to survive to have its own offspring. A deer born with genes that makes it lame will probably not live long enough to mate and have offspring. A predator will likely kill it when it is very young. However, a deer born with genes that help it to run faster than other deer probably will survive and produce offspring. This deer has greater fitness than other deer. If it passes its "speedy" genes on to offspring, they will inherit this useful trait and also will have greater fitness.

Changes in genes happen randomly. Most animals have thousands of genes. Sometimes, the **DNA** that makes up a gene will change. The altered gene may be passed on to offspring. Most of the time, the change has no effect on the offspring or its ability to survive. Sometimes, a change in a gene can decrease fitness, as in the example of the lame deer. Other times, a change in a gene can increase fitness, and make offspring more likely to survive than those who don't have the changed gene.

A change in a gene usually increases fitness when the environment also has changed. For example, suppose that lampreys find their way into a lake that never had lampreys before. The

THE POWER OF A VISUAL FLOWER

The flower of an Australian tongue orchid looks like a female wasp to males. In fact, the male wasp cannot resist landing on this flower and trying to mate with it. As it does, it picks up pollen from the orchid. When it flies to the next orchid and tries to mate with its flower, it transfers the pollen and fertilizes the orchid. As this example shows, in a place where there are many plants competing for the attention of pollinating insects, there is a definite advantage to developing traits that are so attractive to a specific species of insect.

lampreys would parasitize most of the fish, many of which would die. But one fish is born with a changed gene. This change added a terrible-tasting substance to this fish's blood. Lampreys try to parasitize this fish, but because it tastes terrible, they wind up avoiding it. This fish survives and produces offspring. Many of its offspring get the same changed gene, so lampreys avoid them, too. Over time, the descendants of this fish dominate life in the lake, and the lampreys may even die out because of a lack of good-tasting hosts.

What would have happened if lampreys did not invade this lake? In that case, the fish that had the changed gene would not have any benefit over the other fish. The changed gene would not help it in any way. A changed gene helps an organism only if it gives it some survival advantage over other organisms of the same species.

Predators and Prey

Predators and prey influence one another's traits. Predators with traits that help them catch, kill, and eat prey will be successful, and pass on the genes that code for those traits. Of course, prey animals don't want to be eaten. Prey animals with traits that help them get away from predators will pass on the genes that code for those traits. As one trait spreads through a prey population, predators coevolve: Their population changes in response. In this way, predators and prey affect which changed genes are helpful and are passed on from one generation to the next.

Cheetahs are cats that hunt small deerlike animals on the African savanna. The prey can run fast. Over time, faster cheetahs were more successful, and passed on their "speedy" genes. As a species, cheetahs got faster and faster because the fastest ones caught the most prey and produced the most offspring.

As a cheetah runs, it stretches out, bends its back, and then moves its back legs in front of its front legs. This amazing flexibility has made the cheetah the world's fastest land animal.

As the cheetah became faster, the prey evolved ways to avoid the predator. Prey that ran in a zigzag pattern were less likely to be caught. So they were more likely to pass on their genes, including the genes that coded for the zigzag running pattern.

Then, by chance, one cheetah was able to quickly change direction while running. The cheetah that had this ability was a better hunter, survived longer, and passed the genes for this ability on to its offspring. Eventually, all cheetahs zigzagged when they chased prey.

But then, some prey also leapt high in the air while running and zigzagging. It was easier for these prey to avoid being eaten by cheetahs. They were more likely to survive and pass on their genes, including the ones for leaping high in the air.

At some point after that, a cheetah was born that could leap while it was running. This cheetah could more easily catch prey. So this cheetah had more food and could produce more offspring. Over time, all cheetahs were able to leap into the air to grab prey.

Predators and prey are often changing. The changes sometimes help a predator or prey increase its chances of surviving. Predators and prey are agents of change, or evolution, for each other. As one changes, the other often changes in response. This is called coevolution.

It's possible that gene changes might never have given the tiny deer—or other cheetah prey—the ability to zigzag. In that case, cheetahs would not have developed a zigzag running style, either—unless it somehow helped catch more prey. Genes spread through a population when they provide a survival advantage. If there's no survival benefit, the gene will likely not spread.

Competition

Competition for food is also an important agent of evolution. The African savanna contains millions of acres of grassland.

Grazing animals generally do not need to compete with one another for food.

On the other hand, there are not that many trees on the savanna. Browsers—animals that eat tree leaves—must compete with one another for a limited food supply. Some scientists speculate that competition for this food source may have led to the evolution of the giraffe's long neck. Naturalist Charles Darwin and other scientists suggest that the giraffe's long neck may have evolved over time. However, no one really knows for sure how or why the giraffe got its long neck and long legs.

Most browsers on the savanna do not have long necks. They eat low-hanging leaves. A long time ago, giraffes also had short

DARWIN'S FINCHES

During a storm thousands of years ago, one species of bird called finches was blown on the wind or carried on a floating piece of wood from South America to islands in the Pacific Ocean. Some islands had lots of nectar-producing flowers. Others had many seeds and nuts.

Charles Darwin collected 13 species of these birds during his voyage to the Galapagos Islands in the 1830s, but he was unclear about their species. Later researchers returned to the island and sketched images of the birds. All of the finches in the following picture were descended from the original birds that had been blown onto the islands. Over a long period of time, changes in their genes shaped the finches' beaks. Those that ate seeds or nuts had short, strong beaks. Those that ate nectar had long, curved beaks. The researchers found that over time, a single species of finch developed into many different species.

necks. Then, by chance, one giraffe was born with a slightly longer neck. It could eat leaves that were higher on the trees, where other browsers could not reach. This giraffe got more food and could produce more offspring. Over time, these "long-neck" genes continued to change, giving giraffes longer and longer necks. The genes for longer necks were passed on from one generation to the next because they increased the giraffes' fitness. Giraffes with longer necks did not have to compete for food with other animals. Other browsers ate leaves nearer the ground. Only giraffes could eat leaves from the treetops, so giraffes no longer had to compete for food. The giraffes with longer necks could eat more food, avoid competition, survive

1. Geospiza magnirostris. 2. Geospiza fortis.
3. Geospiza parvula. 4. Certhidea olivasea.

Each finch species has a different beak shape that adapts it to eating a certain type of food. Corresponding to the images, these finches eat (1) seeds; (2) buds and fruit; (3) leaves; and (4) insects.

longer, and have more offspring. In this way, a longer neck gave giraffes a survival advantage. It became part of the genes of all giraffes, and today every giraffe has a long neck.

Competition for food has resulted in important changes in many species. For example, scientists suggest that there may have been a time several million years ago when the ancestors of the panda competed with other animals for grasses. Then, by chance, one panda was born with changed genes that enabled its stomach to digest bamboo. This hungry panda may have taken a nibble of bamboo and been able to digest it. This panda's genes were passed on to future generations of pandas. So pandas began to eat a little bamboo, which no other animal could eat. Over a million years or more, many panda genes changed. Some gene changes gave pandas the extremely strong, grinding teeth that helped them chew bamboo. Other genes changed to give pandas a digestive system that could use bamboo as a food. Over time, random changes in the pandas' genes turned them into a species that could survive only on bamboo. By eating bamboo, the pandas no longer had to compete with other animals for food.

In 1994, university scientists discovered several insect species that took specialization to unheard of extremes. These researchers found that some insects can feed only on the plants on which they are born. Thrips, for example, are insects that can feed only on the needles of the pine tree on which they hatched. They are adapted to digesting the particular chemicals and nutrients in just that one tree. Of course, other pine trees are very similar, but their chemicals and nutrients are just different enough to make them inedible by these highly specialized insects. The scientists found that this extreme form of specialization occurs only among organisms that, like insects, reproduce very rapidly. Rapid reproduction allows genes to change quickly to adapt to a highly specific environment. Super-specialist insects are also not very mobile. That is, they don't move around a lot, but are content to live their lives on one plant.

Every species on earth has developed in response to the conditions in its environment. Finding and eating food are crucial to an animal's survival. Feeding has a strong impact on the evolution of animal species.

Glossary

Adapt   To develop traits and behavior that helps an organism survive in its environment

DNA   (deoxyribonucleic acid) A long string of material that makes up genes. DNA contains instructions for making proteins.

Dexterous   Skillful

Echolocation   Sending out sound waves that bounce off objects and return to the sender. Bats and dolphins use echolocation to find food and move around in their environments.

Ecosystem   The environment in which an organism lives, including all other living things, as well as nonliving things, such as soil, rocks, and weather

Enzymes   Proteins that break down food

Evolution   The process in which populations or species change over time, due to interactions between randomly altered genes and environmental changes

Extinct   An extinct species no longer exists

Food web   A complex diagram of the feeding relationships among organisms

Habitat   The part of an ecosystem in which an organism lives

Kernel   The inner part of a nut

Larvae   (singular, *larva*) The "younger" form of some animals, usually insects. Larvae emerge from eggs and undergo extreme changes in appearance before they become mature.

Metabolism   The process of breaking down food into energy, and using that energy or storing it as fat

Nectar   The sweet liquid produced by flowers and eaten by insects, bats, or birds

Offspring   The "children," or young, of animals

Omnivore   An animal that will eat a wide variety of food, including both plant and animal food

Organisms   Living things

Parasite   An organism that lives by using the food that is ingested by its host; in a parasitic relationship, the parasite benefits but the host is harmed.

Passive feeder   An animal that does not actively seek out its food

Photosynthesis   The process in which plants make their own food using the energy in sunlight to change water and carbon dioxide into sugar and oxygen

Plankton   Very tiny, sometimes microscopic, plants and animals that live in water

Pollen   The male sex cells of a flower. Pollen can be compared to the sperm in male animals.

Pollination   The process in which an animal, or other agent such as the wind, carries pollen from one flower to the female part of another flower

Predator   An animal that hunts and eats other animals

Prey   An animal that is hunted and eaten by a predator

Primary producer   Plants that form the base of nearly all food chains and food webs on earth because they do not eat other organisms, but make their own food via photosynthesis

Species   A group of animals that have the same characteristics and that can mate and produce fertile offspring

Bibliography

Attenborough, David. *The Large Mammals*. Princeton, N.J.: Princeton University Press, 2002.

Grice, Gordon. *The Red Hourglass: Lives of the Predators*. New York: Delacorte Press, 1998.

Lippson, Alice Jane and Robert L. Lippson. *Life in the Chesapeake Bay*. Baltimore: The Johns Hopkins University Press, 1984.

McFarland, David, ed. *The Oxford Companion to Animal Behavior*. New York: Oxford University Press, 1981.

Owen, Jennifer. *Feeding Strategy*. Chicago, University of Chicago Press, 1982.

Further Resources

Animal Behavior. Alexandria, VA: Time-Life Books, n/d. ISBN: 0-8094-9658-5

Barre, Michel. *Animals and the Quest for Food*. Milwaukee: Gareth Stevens Publishing, 1998.

Bramwell, Martyn. *Mammals: The Small Plant-Eaters*. New York: Facts on File, 1988.

Fredericks, Anthony D. *Fearsome Fangs*. New York: Franklin Watts, 2002.

Graham, Anna. *Fierce Predators*. New York: Bearport Publishers, 2006.

Hickman, Pamela. *Animals Eating*. Toronto: Kids Can Press, 2001.

Kalman, Bobbie. *How Do Animals Find Food?* New York: Crabtree Publishing, 2001.

Knight, Tom. *Fantastic Feeders*. Chicago: Heinemann, 2003.

Landstrom, Lee Ann & Karen I. Shragg. *Nature's Yucky*. Missoula, Mont.: Mountain Press Publishing, 2003.

Riley, Peter. *Food Chains*. New York: Franklin Watts, 1998.

Swanson, Diane. *Feet that Suck and Feed*. New York: Greystone Books, 2000.

———. *Teeth that Stab and Grind*. New York: Greystone Books, 2000.

Woodward, John, ed. *Extreme Eaters*. New York: Blackbirch/Thomson Gale, 2005.

WEB SITES

Animal Behavior and Ethology

http://cas.bellarmine.edu/tietjen/animal_behavior_and_ethology.htm

A jumping-off point for learning about all aspects of animal feeding and other behaviors.

Animal Defenses against Predators.

http://io.uwinnipeg.ca/~simmons/ysesp/comeco5.htm

This site contains information and pictures that show the different strategies that prey animals use to avoid being eaten by predators.

Animal Planet

http://www.animalplanet.com.au/predators_prey/index.shtml

A brief discussion of the relationship between predators and prey, with links to more information.

Decomposers

http://www.worsleyschool.net/science/files/decomposers/page.html

This Web site contains an informative discussion of decomposers and their important role in ecosystems. The site includes pictures and explanations of the role and behavior of various decomposer species.

Food Chains and Webs

http://www.vtaide.com/png/foodchains.htm

The site contains definitions and discussions of food chains and webs, including diagrams and examples.

Nature Works

http://www.nhptv.org/natureworks/nwep10.htm.

Brief overviews of different feeding habits, including herbivores, carnivores, omnivores, etc. The site also has links to more detailed information about specific animal species.

The Open Door Web Site
http://www.saburchill.com/chapters/chap0015.html
An easy-to-understand discussion of herbivores, what they eat, their
   physiology and behavior.

Predators
Nowhere to Hide. www.science.fau.edu/sharklab/media/bbc/
predators_prog2.html.
An interesting site that briefly discusses predators and then provides
   interesting examples of predatory behavior for different species.

Predator Conservation
The Truth about Predators
http://www.predatorconservation.org/predator_info/
predatorinfo.html
An in-depth look at predators and how they function in an ecosystem. The site has links to information about endangered and
   threatened predators.

Scavengers
http://www.factmonster.com/ipka/A0768543.html
A brief overview of scavengers, including pictures and descriptions
   of specific animal scavengers.

What is an Herbivore?
http://www.qrg.northwestern.edu/projects/marssim/simhtml/
info/whats-a-herbivore.html
This is an informative site with lots of pictures. The site also has
   pages on carnivores, omnivores, decomposers, pollinators, and
   plants.

Picture Credits

Index

About the Author

Natalie Goldstein has been an educational writer for 20 years. She has written numerous publications for young readers on topics such as oceanography, viruses and disease, grassland and forest ecology, and climate change. Goldstein has master's degrees in education and environmental science.